Earl Stanhope

Vindiciæ regiæ, or, a Defence of the Kingly Office

In Two Letters to Earl Stanhope. Second Edition

Earl Stanhope

Vindiciæ regiæ, or, a Defence of the Kingly Office
In Two Letters to Earl Stanhope. Second Edition

ISBN/EAN: 9783337091811

Printed in Europe, USA, Canada, Australia, Japan

Cover: Foto ©ninafisch / pixelio.de

More available books at **www.hansebooks.com**

VINDICIÆ REGIÆ;

OR,

A DEFENCE

OF THE

KINGLY OFFICE.

IN

TWO LETTERS

TO

EARL STANHOPE.

THE SECOND EDITION.

———

LONDON:

PRINTED FOR J. WRIGHT, NO. 169, OPPOSITE
OLD BOND-STREET, PICCADILLY.

1797.

VINDICIÆ REGIÆ, &c.

LETTER I.

My Lord,

If you feel any surprise at all from an address on the subject announced in these Letters, it must be, that it was not sooner made. Indeed, could I have excused to myself an earlier interference, I should long since have remonstrated. But various motives have hitherto restrained me. I will not say that I deemed the nation sufficiently secure from the impression of your sentiments, on account of the violence of their nature, and the want of judgment with which you have maintained them. Unfortunately, extravagance is

B

not always a sure bar to proselytism. But
I did not deem it a duty of mine to interpose.
You might have been more properly an-
swered by others of public situations and
better abilities. Now, however, the question
applies itself to me in a particular manner,
and demands my immediate exertions, if I
would keep the charge entrusted to me,
with that watchfulness which is due to my
sacred office.—Your Lordship discovers me
to be a clergyman.

Will it be matter of mortification or triumph to your Lordship, that at length you
have gained a proselyte to one of the most
pernicious of your opinions?—that proselyte comes from the bosom of my parish,
and affords the immediate cause of this appeal to the director of his sentiments. While
your principles were thrown to the nation
at large, I lamented, but did not take upon
me to confute them. While you addressed
them to the House, I pitied the Peers, indeed,
but held my tongue. Now, at length, you
put yourself in my power.—I find you

within my proper boundary, and set in force my right of complaint against you. The guardian of the Scriptural sentiments of my parishioners, I oppose you on their account, and call you to answer for your trespass of doctrine.

There are several degrees of conviction, into the production of which both the ability of the persuader and the candour of the party addressed will jointly enter. The highest kind is that which triumphs over an opposite prejudice.—Truth is so advantageously proposed, as to extort acquiescence from unwilling-ness itself. This is highly honourable to the powers of the pleader ; nor is it with-out a certain commendation to the consent-ing person : for truth is always so valuable, that not to be obstinately blind to it, is the ground of some good opinion.—The next, or middle kind, is that which succeeds to a state of *indifference.* I speak in the philo-sophical sense of the word. Here the mind rests on its general powers of discernment ;

and either free from all previous impression as to the particular case to be examined, or, by an express exertion, removing it during the discussion, waits upon the evidence with a disengaged attention, and judges with wisdom and composure, because it was not pre-occupied. The lowest degree, is that which follows a previous inclination: here the mind, longing to fortify itself in a given opinion, eagerly and inconsiderately lays hold of whatever may tend to promote it ; and thus may followers be made in the greatest numbers, without assistance from any truth or ability at all.—May Heaven grant me to be ever in the middle of these classes :—my parishioner I know to be in the last of them, with respect to your Lordship's doctrine.—Shall I find yourself in the first ?—Oh ! that my powers were equal to the victorious statement of irresistible truth ! —Oh ! that your mind were not too deeply pledged to the maintenance of inveterate error !

My Lord, you have indirectly declared, in

your place in Parliament,* and my parishioner believes you—that the Kingly Office is forbidden by the Scriptures. This you
infer from a particular passage, which must
be quoted at length, that the argument to
arise from it may be the better seen.

In answer to a demand of the Israelites,
that Samuel, who had hitherto governed
them with the title of Judge, would appoint
a King over them, the Prophet endeavours
to dissuade them from their purpose by giv-
ing the following portrait of their King :†

Ver. 11. " This will be the manner of the
" King that shall reign over you. He will
" take your sons, and appoint them for
" himself, for his chariots, and to be his
" horsemen ; and some shall run before his
" chariots.

12. " And he will appoint him captains
" over thousands, and captains over fifties ;
" and will set them to ear his ground, and
" to reap his harvest, and to make his

" instruments of war, and instruments of his
" chariots.

13. " And he will take your daughters
" to be confectionaries, and to be cooks, and
" to be bakers.

14. " And he will take your fields, and
" your vineyards, and your olive yards,
" even the best of them, and give them to
" his servants.

15. " And he will take the tenth of your
" seed, and of your vineyards, and give to
" his officers, and to his servants.

16. " And he will take your men-servants,
" and your maid-servants, and your good-
" liest young men, and your asses, and put
" them to his work.

17. " He will take the tenth of your
" sheep ; and ye shall be his servants.

18. " And ye shall cry out in that day,
" because of your King which ye shall have
" chosen you ; and the Lord will not hear
" you in that day."

Had you asserted that this terrible description belonged principally, if not ex-

clusively, to the King of the Israelites, you would have experienced no contradiction from me. But as Parliament is not a school of doctors sitting for the purpose of criticism on Jewish history ; and the Constitution supposes, that whatever is there uttered is applicable to the circumstances of the state, your only object must have been to make a sweeping conclusion ; which, attaching to the cause of Kings at large, must of course go to affect the maintenance of Royalty among ourselves ; and by one stretch of your disaffected logic, a Rehoboam or a Manasseh is unawares connected in iniquity and unlawfulness with George the Third.—
I hope to shew you, and my too credulous parishioner, the monstrous error of this opinion : only premising, that as you have yourself appealed to Scripture for the establishment of your argument, I shall try you by the same standard, drawing from thence the bulk of my reasoning, secure of any interruption, which, as an unbeliever in

other respects, you might be inclined to give me.

1. What if I observe to you, at our entrance on the subject, that the description before us proves by far too little to answer the views you have in quoting it. You imagine, I dare say, that it means to convey the idea of the orderly process of all regal authority—that it is a faithful representation of Kings as they ever were, and ever must be. No such thing. There are some restraining circumstances belonging to it, about which I must beg to give your Lordship a little information.—I will not detain you with the different opinions as to the word which is translated " manner" in the above passage : you may be assured from Grotius, that it contains a distinction between the real rights of sovereignty, and the accidental excesses of them—between the principle of royalty *(jus regium)* and its occasional practice. You may also be assured of this by comparing the Bible with

itself—by viewing an orderly King described by Moses, together with the terrible one
threatened by Samuel.*　The possible extravagance of the Kingly Office must therefore be carefully separated from its regular
process; and this is one of the points which
I meant to distinguish.　Nor is this all.—It
was not a usual King, with the common
chances of his good or bad government,
whom the Israelites were to serve:—their
demand of a King had (for reasons which I
will shew you by and by) incurred the dis-
pleasure of Heaven ; they were therefore
to be punished, in an appropriate manner,
through the wickedness of their sovereigns.
These were to be raised up by God, as the
peculiar instruments of his vengeance ; and
their conduct, operating widely from the
usual administration of Royalty, was desti-
ned to accomplish the dreadful, but deserved
chastisement.　This was the foundation of
Samuel's menaces.　If you doubt it, turn to

* Deut. xvii. 14—20.

the subsequent history of the Israelites, and you will find his predictions abundantly verified in the scourging rule of Rehoboam,* Manasseh, Amon,† Ahab,‡ and others. If you still doubt, turn to the prophet Hosea||, who introduces the Deity declaring his own purposes in this appointment :—" I " gave thee a King in my wrath."—We see then the futility of your argument: for the description in question applies not to the orderly process of regal government, but is meant to hold out the image of a *vindictive King*, acting on a peculiar commission. And thus is the Regal Office in general rescued from your censure.

But there is a farther point, in which you are to be instructed. I have said that the words of Samuel, so far from being descriptive of the regular authority of common Kings, must be understood of a vindictive sovereign.—What if I add, that, together with this pernicious conduct of the native

* 1 Kings iv. 12. † 2 Kings xxi. ‡ 1 Kings xxi. || Ch. xiii. 11.

rulers, they comprehend the destruction of the Israelitish polity by the Babylonish conquest, and foretell the cruel treatment of the Hebrews by Nebuchadnezzar.

I entreat your attention to the following particulars, which will shew you the principle of this assertion :

The prophetic parts of the Scripture are written in a manner which, if you are a Scripture reader, you will readily acknowledge, and which is equally true, whether you acknowledge it or not ;—sometimes the events of future ages are foretold in a simple and direct way ; whether with or without the full comprehension of them by the inspired writers themselves, matters not in this inquiry : the objects are pointed out in their own situation, not to be perceived till the lapse of time shall have made a long train of circumstances conspire together for the production of the promised effect. Then, the whole of the heavenly plan becomes so rounded by the providential direction of things, and is made so striking to the eye of the rational interpreter, that, looking from the completed fact before him to the ancient page which announced it, he declares the prediction to be fulfilled, and justifies the prescience of God by the efficient, though unsuspecting, concurrence of man.

Of this kind I will refer you only to two instances, *instar omnium :* the naming of Cyrus,* and Josiah,† the one a hundred, the other upwards of three hundred years before his birth.

This, as I said, is the more direct kind of prophecy. There is another to be mentioned. Sometimes the prediction is not thus sparing of immediate impression. Looking forward, indeed, like the former, to some future event, but connecting it with another that is less remote (on account of certain secret ties which bind both subjects together) through the narration of one it points out the intention of the other, and involves two

* Isaiah xliv. 28. † 1 Kings xiii. 2.

facts, separate in point of time, under the same terms, or glances at both with alternate signification. The proximate action, soon to commence, is stamped with the character of the ultimate one in farther prospect ; and a mutual and intimate blending of a double subject, takes place under the apparent terms of one description. I could tell you how things of a less visible relation are thus compelled to serve together in the mysteries of the Divine prescience. I could tell you how a spiritual event (the greatest that can happen to mortals) is foretold under the immediate cast and colour of a temporal one; how the terrors of the last judgment are anticipated through the approaching destruction of Jerusalem.* But my business is with the prophecy of Samuel, all the parts of which are of similar natures. The whole is political. The proximate event is the punishment of the Israelites, by the rule of Kings purposely vindictive : the ultimate

* Matthew xxiv.

one is, the cruelty they are to experience from a foreign conqueror. As if he had said, " Since ye rebel against the authority " of your proper sovereign (God), and pre- " fer the earthly rule of Kings ; through " Kings shall come the characteristic chas- " tisement of your defection. Your native " Kings shall be made to rule you with pe- " culiar severity ; and (what is more) ye " shall be carried into captivity by the King " of Babylon ; to whom ye should never " have been subjected, if ye had preserved " your bounden allegiance to your ancient " governor." I could quote the opinion of Houbigant and others to this effect. If you still doubt, I beg you to compare the fol- lowing passages with the terms of the de- scription in question : 2 Chronicles xxxvi. 20. Isaiah xxxix. 6. 7. an the 1st chapter, 3d verse, &c. of Daniel, who was himself of the number of the captives.—Thus then is the fury to be exerted in the moment of con- quest by a foreign enemy, connected with the peculiarity of their native sovereignty already pointed out. And yet, you take the whole to be the representation of a common King in Judea, and, by consequence, of a common King in any other country, and therefore that they are to be all proscribed together !—For shame, my Lord !—correct the ignorance or the misrepresentation with which you labour. If you do not respect the religious principle, on which I would exhort you and every person to interpret the Bible, yet do it for your credit's sake, as a man of education, exerting his attention on an important volume of ancient history.

2. I have hitherto viewed the argument in a light different, *ab initio*, from your Lordship. I will now contend with you more on your own ground. I will drop the peculiarity belonging to it, and allow, for the sake of discussion, that the description of the Israelitish Kingship is nothing else than that of the authority acquired by the Eastern princes in general. More than this it is impossible to concede ; nor have

any of the commentators supposed that, in
its largest sense, the quotation involves any
thing farther. But what then? your inference is as illogical as if this were not so;
for where is the connection proper for your
purpose? Because the attachment of the
Eastern nations has always leaned towards
Monarchy in its absolute sense, and because
they have always endured what may appear
to you to be intolerable oppression under
that form of government; are we therefore
oppressed because we too have a Monarch,
but with limitations of his authority?—On
the contrary, is not our own possession of
liberty indirectly proved (if to an Englishman an indirect proof were necessary) by
the keen sense we affect of the miseries of
those, who, in their own opinion, may ne-
vertheless be contented and happy? Aristotle was a man of some judgment; and,
one should think, might be credited as soon
as any of those who cannot " sleep o'nights,"
because of the supposed slavery of they

know not what remote people. Aristotle expressly tells you, that the Asiatics of his days (not altered, you may depend, to the present hour) had no objection to their form of government, despotic as it was.* But what if this were not so? is the single name of Monarchy to identify every branch and species of it, which the mighty difference of situation and manners has struck out in so great a variety through the world? Are the offices of all sovereigns commutable? will the same degree of power follow the same outward title? and (if their ages would have permitted it) might the Monarch George and the Monarch Nebuchadnezzar have exchanged thrones, without any interruption of their respective sentiments?—I will not venture to suppose what his surprise would be at the inconvenient claims of the constitution against him: but how

---

* Ὁι περι την Ασιαν ὑπομενυσι την δεσποτικην αςχην, ὐδεν δυσχεραινονίες.

C

would his Babylonish Majesty have stared at the discovery of a Democrat Peer?—In your senatorial capacity at least, if not in your new employment of teaching political divinity, it might be expected that you should look with more discrimination on the various essence of civil authorities even of the same name. But you, ignorantly or wilfully, confound every shade and line of true distinction ; and all that is not written in the characters of Democracy, is, in the eye of your aversion, nothing but one vast blot of insupportable tyranny.

I deem my argument to be good against you. However, I will confess an anxiety as to one part of it. My Lord, let us draw a little nearer. It is true, the King is neither an Ahab, nor a Nebuchadnezzar. Good man ! his nature and his office together make him as " innocent as a Doge of Venice."* Neither does he " take our fields

* " Innocente quanto un Doge di Venezia." This is the Italian proverb for innoxious authority. Yet the

and give them to his servants ;" nor are our " sons made eunuchs in his palace." But there is a certain part of the description before us, in which he may have exerted his tyranny, and justified the prophecy of Samuel. I would ask, has he verified the beginning of the 13th verse, in prejudice of your family ?—the word " confectionaries" in that passage, is, in other places of Scripture, written " apothecaries." They are equivalent terms, and are indifferently rendered by our translators from the same original. Thus in ch. xxx. of Exodus, ver. 25. an " ointment is said to be compound after " the art of the apothecary." I tremble at the pernicious discovery I have made against myself—but it must out, though my argument suffer from it. The verse in question must therefore be read thus : " and he will " take your daughters to be apothecaries."

Democrats have not failed to cry over Manini himself, " The Tyrant is gone, &c."—Happy union of ignorance and lies!

I am the more confirmed in this, because the word translated " bakers" in the same verse, still looks to the preparation of confectionary wares, or (which is the same thing) apothecary's wares, and comes from a word which means, to "*pound as it were in a mortar.*—

But I check the indulgence of this strain ; for (whatever be the temptation to it) I have no intention to treat your Lordship with levity.

3. I now proceed to state a circumstance, which, after what you have asserted, will perhaps startle you, *viz.*—That the government of the Israelites had been a regal one from the beginning, and that the passage in question, reprobating such a King as was requested of Samuel, was in perfect consonance with their original sovereignty, and necessarily resulted from it.

There are two kinds of divine supremacy with respect to man ;—one general, the other special. One flows from the standing

relation between the Creator and his creatures, the other from some separate and peculiar purpose. To the former is given the
name of the " natural sovereignty" of God ;
(monarchia naturalis) to the latter, that of
his " civil dominion" *(monarchia civilis)*.
Of the former species of rule, the world at
large are the subjects, of the latter, have
been the Hebrews alone. If you doubt this,
go to the Old Testament, the general tenour
of which abundantly declares the divine nature of the Hebrew government: go to
the Christian writers on the affairs of that
people, who uniformly acknowledge it : go
to Josephus himself, who, discarding all
other names characteristic of the various
modes of civil rule, assumes for it the appropriate title of a *Theocracy.*

It is impossible to resolve all this into
the common superintendence of God over
the concerns of his creatures. In a certain
sense, indeed, all governments are divine, the
tendency of which is the standing good of

man ; for Heaven has sanctioned, on num-
berless occasions, the establishment of wholesome authorities for the sake of social happiness and a virtuous tranquillity.   In this
acceptation, "the powers that be, are or-
dained of God :"—and I beg to remind your
Lordship and others, that the disturbance of
these salutary powers involves not only a
political, but a religious offence, and is an
outrage to Heaven as well as to earth.   But
it is not in so remote a sense that the divine
government of the Israelites is affirmed.
Theirs was an immediate control mani-
fested in various shapes—sometimes by a
direct display of celestial glory to the eyes
of the people at large,*—sometimes by the
selection of certain among them as the instruments of communication to the rest†—
and always by supernatural power exerted
over the whole of their transactions, in-
fluencing them, as the Deity thought fit,
in every matter of peace or war.‡   In short,

* Exod. xiii. 21. † Exod. xix. 7. ‡ Deut. iv. 7.

their actual ruler was a divine King, and the apparent administrators of the affairs of the Hebrews were mere agents to this celestial sovereign, appointed by his primary selection, and dismissed, if their disaffected conduct required it, by the interference of his imperial authority. And this, if you will but look into their history, you will find to attach to them in all situations, whether under the earlier guidance of their Elders and Judges, when the Theocracy was in full action over them ; or under the forbidden Kings themselves ; though the appointment of the latter gave a wound to the Divine Supremacy, and occasioned a gradual and resentful diminution of it towards them.

Here then is the material question to be asked. Upon what principle did the Prophet utter that reprobation of an Israelitish King, which you are willing to believe is a divine bar to the establishment of Royalty any where ?—I answer, that it was the local

consequence of such an appointment. The
Hebrews had a King already. The learned
Spencer (I shall mention him again by and
by) will prove to you, that God exercised
his sovereignty among them in the most
convincing manner.* Gideon told this truth
to them, when they wished to obey a King
in his own person.† And, in the transaction immediately before us, God himself
indignantly speaks of them as subjects guilty
of defection from him, " They have not
" rejected thee," says he to Samuel, " but
" they have rejected *me*, that *I* should not
" reign over them."‡ You see then the
guilt of the proposed measure. It went
either to the causeless rejection of the existing sovereignty, or to the creation of a
double and a clashing authority. It was
impious or unreasonable;—impious, because it led to a revolt from their proper

---

* Deum potestatem vere regalem inter Hebræos ha-
buisse.

† Judges viii. 22, 23.　　‡ 1 Samuel viii. 7.

King, who had hitherto protected them by miraculous power;—unreasonable, because it formed a supernumerary office, and exhibited two Kings acting at once over the same people. Now let us try your Lordship's inference by this standard, applying it to the civil powers of the present day. We acknowledge the Divine Authority, through the permission of which our own form of Monarchical government is established; but it is in the general and less peculiar acceptation of Divine Authority which I first defined. In this nation therefore the King is the primary governor.—A Theocracy never having obtained here. He is, indeed, together with other men, responsible to God for the execution of the trust reposed in him; but in his quality of Civil Ruler, he is to us what the Deity was to the Hebrews. In order then to draw the desired parallel between the two cases, some discontented or absurd person must propose either to reject *in toto* the present sovereignty of the House of Brunswick, in spite of their blameless government over us, or to set up an Assessor of his Majesty's throne, trenching on his peculiar prerogatives, and aspiring to share with him the management of his proper authority. Shew me the man, whose wickedness or weakness may lead him to this attempt, and I will join issue with your Lordship in assailing him with Scriptural denunciations. Till then I must take the liberty of differing from you : and while I contend that the general establishment of Kingly authority is safe from your Democratic inference, I hope to have convinced you, that the Prophet's reprobation attaches to the peculiar case of an Israelitish King, and on the principle which I have just stated.

Perhaps I have said enough as to the singularity attaching to the sovereignty of the Israelites. It was strictly a singularity, and incommunicable to any other state. I will now proceed,

4. To add a few words on the general doctrine of the Scriptures concerning Kings; that our own Christian situation may be connected with this Hebrew discussion, and that you and my parishioner may no longer think yourselves at liberty to apply to the sovereigns of the present day, that denunciation which the Prophet, on peculiar grounds, uttered against the demand of a King by the Israelites.

I will not, with some, look into Paradise for the divine institution of Kingship. I will satisfy myself with pointing out to you the more remote, yet effectual, sanction of its expediency. This I find in the general, I had almost said the universal, prevalence of that species of authority, as soon as mankind became sufficiently numerous to allow a separation of communities. The regularity of social institution will, in this case, be the voice of God. The powers and propensities of man were evidently cast by his Creator for that species of government, and, as soon as circumstances permitted him, he obeyed the impulse by erecting the dominion of Kings. The description of the early state of mankind which the Bible affords, in connection with the history of the chosen people, is of great importance in this matter. Wherever casual mention is made of the Gentile governments (and you may be the more convinced by this very casualty) they are Royal governments. Whether in Shinar or Egypt, the same Abram finds an Amraphel* or a Pharaoh. When the Hebrews arrive at their land of promise, it is full of Kings ; and at the time of the transaction, concerning which we dispute, the whole of the East is administered by Kings. This is evident from the words of the Israelites themselves, who, looking to the example of their neighbours, demand a King " like ALL the nations."†

If your Lordship is tempted to object, that the lawfulness of Kings cannot be

* Gen. xiv. 1.   † Ver. 20.

proved by their mere existence, for moral
evil has always existed, and may be de-
fended on the same ground ; I answer, that
there is the greatest difference imaginable
between an avowed institution and accidental practice. Regular establishments
(especially such as may be traced through
the whole history of man) are always
formed on a supposed good. They profess
to have a standing salutary object in view.
Now, moral evil was never an institution :
though unhappily found every where, it
is an unlicensed and ever-shifting principle,
lurks in corners till it may come forth with
impunity, acts by fits and starts, as the vigi-
lance or remissness of public virtue tends to
repress or indulge it, and every where betrays its permitted nature but unsanctioned
agency. Shew me among what people
moral evil was ever set up by national appointment, and continued by public authority through successive generations, and
I resign my argument. Till then, believe

with me, that the two points are *toto cælo*
distinct, and that the open and general government of Kings, from the earliest re-
cords of history to the present time, shews
the conveniency of that office to the welfare of man, and the developement of God's
original designs, in the standing institutions
of his creatures.

If you should not relish this Scriptural
derivation of Kings, I could shew you, if it
lay fairly in my way, that profane history
equally points them out as springing from
the nature of man. People of your Lordship's way of thinking, will perhaps affect
to prefer the latter kind of evidence. Whether Polybius obtains a more effectual attention from your party than Moses, I will
not undertake to say ; but fortunately either
of them will answer my purpose. Turn then
to the circle of governments described in the
fragments of his 6th book. He begins with
natural Monarchy. This, according to him,
is the first species of rule known to man, and

soon ameliorates itself into a beneficial and well understood Royalty. From this salutary point, he describes the factious progress of Oligarchy—of Aristocracy—of Democracy—and Ochlogarchy ; in which last state, government becomes so impracticable, that, in order to subsist at all, it must immediately return to its first principle. You see, my Lord, how near your favourite government is to the *end* of this cycle of authorities. Even in Polybius's hands (who makes it respectable and select in comparison of the projects of you and your party) it stands just before the *point of extreme confusion,* the *universal empire of the mob;* from whence he declares that Monarchy must begin over again, the mobbish principle being too violent and too absurd to be long-lived, and the rule of all, naturally resolving itself into that of one. You see that I can answer the purpose of my argument from both quarters. And what is it but truth, which manifests itself thus universally ! Reason and Scripture agree in the convenience of Regal authority to the guidance of the world ; and " Agamemnon " King of men," pleads as loudly against you as " Tidal, King of nations."*

If you are disposed to dwell on the cause of Republics, I answer that their convenience to the welfare of man does not so fully appear from history. Comparatively speaking, it is but an insignificant portion of the world which had ever obeyed that form of government ; nor do the internal tumults necessarily resulting from those institutions, allow them in general to be either happy or long-lived. They have been for the most part capricious and ill-fated experiments upon the original government. They have grown out of Monarchy, and, after insulting their parent for a while, have sunk into Monarchy again. There has been of late much triumphant and ignorant quotation of the example of Rome—But what is the genuine conclusion to be drawn from

* Gen. xiv. i.

its history? Assuredly not a Republican one. If we suppose a total period of 1200 years from the building of the city to the extinction of the Western empire, what portion of it will be occupied by the Republic?—about one third ; and even during that short time, the course of the Democracy was suspended by occasional Dictatorships, which every extraordinary pressure of affairs rendered necessary. What again of Greece, which has afforded its share of exultation to the modern innovators? its Republics rose like that of Rome. " Kings" were also their " nursing fathers." It is true, they did not, as Rome did, fall back into the bosom of their ancient parent. They suffered for it. Persisting in the indulgence of their new and wayward system, they sunk under the evils which it naturally engendered ; they were first torn in pieces by internal dissensions, and from a domestic weakness ignominiously passed to a foreign subjection.—But I return to my Bible. It is in my power to prove more

D

than the indication of the **Regal Office** through the nature of man. The Scriptures represent the frequent employment of Kings, in execution of the purposes of Heaven, so as to demonstrate that they were not unholy or forbidden things *ab initio*. Thus (to spare you other instances) Cyrus is described as raised up for the deliverance of the Hebrews from their Babylonish captivity. If you object again, that moral evil is frequently made subservient to the Divine views with respect to man, I agree with you, and bless that Providence which can deprive mischief of its sting, and compel it to perform a salutary service foreign to its nature. But I must refer you again to an essential distinction between the two cases : the one is apparently left to its own spontaneous agency, and in its malignant attempt to disturb the settled progress of good, is suddenly deflected from its aim by the watchful control of Heaven : the other is looked forward to, and relied upon, as the standing means of agency in

the constitutional order of things. To illustrate this, take an instance, the strongest
you could wish for your argument. Compare
the case of Job with that of Cyrus, to whom
I have already referred you. Satan, in
whom the evil principle is personified, assaults the Patriarch with temptations, di-
vinely permitted. But how?—is he authori-
tatively called to this employment by any
solemn selection? No. He thrusts himself
forward unbidden, to thwart the temporal
happiness, and, through it, the religious
obedience, of the servant of God. It is only
after repeated solicitations that he is allowed
to accomplish the afflictions of Job; and
after all, the effect is totally contrary to his
wishes, and to temporary appearances.—
What now of Cyrus?—is he thus left to
make his appearance uncalled for and un-
authorized? on the contrary, he is anticipated by the sacred voice of prophecy. His
Kingly power is necessary to the production
of the promised event. This is manifest

from the declaration of his own designs.*
He is called the " Shepherd of the Lord,
" who shall perform all his pleasure,"—the
" Anointed of the Lord, whose right hand he
" hath holden,"—" raised up by the Lord
" in righteousness, who would direct all his
" ways."† What now does your Lordship
think? would all these preparations be made
for the introduction of an unholy or forbidden thing? Oh, no. Was ever moral evil
thus magnificently anticipated? was ever
the malignant principle thus sanctioned with
heavenly regard? Again I say, no.

But I am not left to the mere force of an
inference, however strong. There are the
most positive precepts, in every part of the
Scriptures, enjoining respectful obedience to
the powers then existing. These powers
were Regal; and whatever your opinion
may be as to the tyranny prevailing in
them, and the unlawfulness of their natures,

* Ezra i. 2.   † Isaiah xliv. xlv.

the divine will was, that they should receive
a cheerful and a conscientious submission. I
will state an extreme case to you, by which
you may judge of the rest. In the most dis-
astrous circumstances, not amid the rule of
their native princes, but even in a state of
captivity, the Hebrews are commanded by
God to acquiesce in their situation,—nay,
to assist with their prayers the very empire
that held them in subjection. Do you think
this incredible? Hear the solemn injunction
of God to the Israelites, through the Prophet
Jeremiah.—" Seek ye the peace of the city,
" whither I have caused you to be carried
" away captive, and *pray unto the Lord for*
" it: *for in the peace thereof ye shall have*
" *peace."** A most important lesson ! And
if this was binding in the most calamitous
of political conditions—the power of the
conqueror on one side, and nothing but submission on the other,—how much more

* Ch. xxix. 7.

ought it to constrain you, and all those whose happiness it is (if you would but acknowledge it) to live under the mildest and best of governments; the fixed principles of which secure you from all oppression, and under whose well-balanced supremacy your duties and your rights go hand in hand, and beautifully illustrate and support each other!

The New Testament is full of the same precepts, applying, some of them, to times not much more favourable to the ease of the subject than those before mentioned. However, both public and private subjection are enjoined " for conscience sake." All servants are required, by St. Paul, to " obey " their masters according to the flesh ;"* and St. Peter, mentioning the Regal Office as the most comprehensive name for sovereignty at large, bids the Christians scattered through the East, to submit, for the Lord's sake, to " every ordinance of man ;"

* Coloss. iii. 22.

that is, to every mode and form of regal authority there prevailing,—whether to Kings (as if no other species of rule were necessary to be stated), or to Governors, deputed by their imperial authority.* The Saviour himself exhibited in his own conduct the deep sense he entertained of the conscientious obedience due to the Regal Power under which he passed his earthly life. While he preserved inviolate the majesty of God, he adjudged to Cæsar the rights of Cæsar; † and, rather than afford any pretext of faction to his followers, he performed a miracle in order to pay a tax required under a system upheld by a King. ‡ Would the Scriptures have been thus respectful, do you think, to an institution unholy in itself, and forbidden *in rerum naturâ?* would the power of Heaven have been called in to maintain any species of earthly authority radically vicious, and inherently evil?—If you want any far-

* Coloss. ii. 13.   † Matt. xxii. 21.   ‡ Matt. xvii. 27.

ther example to convince you, take that of the first ages of Christianity, and in the words of a writer whom I recommend to your conscientious perusal. "There is scarce-
" ly any particular instance wherein primi-
" tive Christianity did more triumph in the
" world, than in their exemplary obedience
" to the powers and magistrates under which
" they lived, honouring their persons, rever-
" ing their power, and paying them tri-
" bute," &c.*

I believe I have now said enough to convince—I will not say your Lordship,—but any reader not hardened by prejudice. If you are not yet satisfied, and should you be really desirous of informing yourself on a sacred subject, I will farther beg to recommend to you a small tract on the Jewish Theocracy, written by a most learned countryman of our own, whom I have already named. Your bookseller will send you Spen-

* Cave Prim. Christ. Part III. C. 4.

cer on the Hebrew Ritual, in the first volume
of which you will find the dissertation of
which I speak. It cannot fatigue you.—It
is comprized in less than thirty of his pages,
(I hope you are not afraid of a folio page);
and when you have perused it, you may
wish, perhaps, that some friend had pointed
it out to you before you ventured your Scriptural critique to the Peers. Hitherto, I fear,
the Scriptures have obtained but little of
your genuine attention. I say this presump-
tively, I confess : not that I have had an opportunity of gathering it from any personal
knowledge of your Lordship, but because,
in your use of the passage in question, you
seem to have no collateral acquaintance with
the Bible, by which to interpret it. It has the
appearance of being to you a solitary and
independent quotation, which you have stum-
bled upon by accident, and which, at the
first cursory reading, charmed you with the
handle it afforded for a democratic inference,
drawn from what you inwardly knew to be

a book of the highest and most awful authority. Perhaps you pleased yourself with the thought of quelling the Bishops on their own ground!—how must they have smiled at your ignorance, if they did not weep over your perverseness! There is another thing which persuades me, though in a more remote degree, of your general want of acquaintance with the Scriptures—I find others who profess your way of thinking, remarkably ignorant of the Bible, concerning which, however, they will venture the strongest assertions. Your convert, and my parishioner, is of this class. He knows, and is determined to know, nothing more of it than what you have taught him. All the rest is but blotted paper. I pray God to pardon his error, or to subdue his obstinacy!

I will take this opportunity of saying, that on no other subject do I observe so much arrogance joined with so much ignorance. In the several departments of knowledge, the well-instructed generally take upon them

the task of information; or if an incompe-
tent person will now and then step forward,
he assumes what appearance he can of intelligence, and his very insufficiency is made
to pay homage to true science. The modest
not unfrequently keep silence, when it might
be of signal advantage if they would risk
themselves a little : but the totally uninform-
ed, *plane indocti*, are sure to refrain. What
of the science of the Scriptures? Here all is
changed. It is the boast of its enemies, not
to know the Bible, and to pronounce it not
worth their knowing ; to vilify what they
have never examined, what they profess
they never will examine; or (the worst case
of all), to turn hastily to it for a pernicious
purpose, and to strengthen the general dis-
belief of the ignorant and the profligate, by
the perfidious appearance of a legitimate inquiry. The ignorant leader of this unphi-
losophical multitude boasts that he possessed
no Bible of his own. How did he contrive
to write against it ? He once borrowed a

Bible in order to look into it, and refute it ! ! !
In the name of learning, what other branch
of study is thus conducted? Did Bentley
once borrow a Phalaris to prove it spurious?
did Polignac once borrow a Lucretius, to
correct his doctrine of God and Nature?
and you too, my Lord, however unversed
in the Scriptures at large, can take into
your hands the sacred volume to answer a
purpose, and to make converts. But shall
I tell you a thought of mine ?—I do believe
then (without wishing to be uncharitable)
that your knowledge of the passage in
question came not originally from the Bible.
I imagine it to have been derived from a
book in which your doctrine is so full blown,
that it fairly betrays the alliance between
you.* That book professes to recite the
crimes of the Queens of France, and was
written in the worst of times, to hasten the

* The title is "Les Crimes des Reines de France,
depuis le commencement de la Monarchie jusqu'à Marie
Antoinette."

fate of the last unfortunate Princess. Whatever scattered evil had been committed, or
imputed, during the entire succession from
Basine to Antoinette is malignantly crowded
together into a small compass. The figures
of some of them in their most offensive
actions are engraved, in order to assist the
impression intended to be made on the eyes
of the ignorant; and the conclusion from the
whole is, that there ought to be no more
Queens, and consequently, no more Kings.
He connects them all in one common proscription in his preface, where he quotes the
very passage of Samuel which you seem to
have taken up from him. He supposes, as
you do, that it attaches to all Kings in every
age and country, and kindly furnishes an
additional speech to the Prophet, who, it
seems, had not been sufficiently comprehensive in his denunciation. " But what, O
" Israelites, if this King of yours, already
" so detestable, will proceed to have a
" Queen too?"—Then follows a black list

of enormities to be committed in emulation, as it were, by the partner of the throne. And thus are the peculiar views of Scripture (which I have endeavoured to explain to you) turned from their proper purpose, and applied to the general cause of Royalty, in order to serve the ignorance and virulence of Jacobinism. I shall be glad if I am not founded in this conjecture as to the source of your Scripture knowledge. I shall be truly relieved to find that it is only an un-acquaintance with your subject which ex-poses you, and that the malignant part of it belongs elsewhere.

With this wish I close the first part of my Address to you, reserving for another Letter a few collateral observations, which, though arising from the main subject, may with more propriety obtain a separate state-ment.

I am, &c.

LETTER II.

My Lord,

There are various modes of invading the Kingly Power. Assaults on the throne must change their appearance in proportion as civilization advances, and political liberty is ascertained. Hence the sole power of the sword in one age, and the preparatory influence of the pen in another; hence what was mere personal consideration between the sovereign and the subject, becomes in time an appeal to principles and opinions. It is a dismal truth, that the class of society which begins immediately from the throne, and stops before it arrives at the people, have generally been the first agitators of rebellion.—And their employment of the mob is always seen to adapt itself to existing circumstances. In the early periods of our history the great malcontents, with little or no management of the vulgar, led them to an immediate attack on the hated sovereign. Thus the Confessor was assailed by Earl Godwin, and Henry VII. by Lord Lovel; and at a later period (but ere yet the Constitution was fixed) Shaftesbury depended more on ten thousand of his " brisk boys," than on the previous management of public opinion. But in an advanced state of public liberty, if the crown is to be attacked, a more circuitous mode becomes necessary. Baronial influence is now lessened, and individual opinions have their weight. Much diligence must therefore be used to corrupt the minds of the people, ere they can be fitted for the required purpose. Hence come the inflammatory doctrines of the present discontented great—hence the emboldened deliberations of the seditious vulgar. The

Godwins and Lovels give place to the Stan-
hopes, and Oxfords ; and the " brisk boys,"
converted into Paines and Thelwalls, take
the field with the " Rights of Man," &c. in
one hand, and the sword in the other. In
the first instance, the mob is the arm to
strike ; in the second, it is also the mouth to
clamour.—But the ultimate consequence is
the same. The same too are the original
views of their great employers, however
different the means of accomplishing them.
These men are the giants of society, making
various war upon the sovereign Gods. Some
of them boldly scale heaven, and attempt
to pluck Jupiter at once from his throne.
Others previously *stoop to the earth to take
up rubbish*, with which to knock down the
celestials.—One common crime of rebellion
involves them all.

To something of this principle I attribute
your interpretation of the passage which
gave occasion to my first Letter. There is
another opinion flowing from the same

E

source, the current of which I shall now endeavour to "dam up." If a King is to be proscribed, it naturally follows that a Republic is the only true government. Accordingly, we hear from your party nothing but the praise of the French Republic, its virtues, and the universal empire which awaits it. Rome, with all its glories and conquests, is introduced to convince us by its example ; and we are taught, that what the conduct of our literary education has held up to our reverence from antiquity, is once more brought round by the concurrence of events, to excite the admiration of the present age. This is the assertion against which I shall employ a few of my concluding pages.

Perhaps there are people whom one general idea may satisfy on a subject however large and complicated—to whose minds Rome and Virtue are equivalent terms, and who regard genuine Liberty and French Republicanism as one and the same thing.—

This summary way of thinking is not always the effect of incurable ignorance; it proceeds more frequently from an indolence capable of better things. To such dispositions I would suggest the propriety of a farther inquiry. This would end in the discovery both of a certain resemblance, and a certain dissimilitude, between the two examples. But what is the dissimilitude? and what the resemblance?—I will point out to your Lordship a few leading particulars of both, on which, as it seems to me, the greatness and virtue of a nation will much depend. I beg you to mark the mighty difference between the Roman and French Republics, with regard to national policy in the treatment of Kings.

I need not remind you of the band of French assassins once proposed to be organized for the murder of all foreign Kings, wherever guilty of reigning. I will only mention the Oath of Hatred to Royalty, which is actually in force by the present laws, and is an indispensable qualification in every legislator. It would be something tolerable if this oath were restricted in terms to the people that have resolved to enforce it. But no. The Frenchman, with singular modesty, sees all mankind in himself; and he swears roundly and universally. The oath comprehends *all* Royalty. Now compare, I beseech you, the wiser Romans with these madmen. Are you ignorant that one of the established functions of the Roman Senate was expressly to confer the title of King on whoever seemed to be worthy of that honour? Whatever their real persuasions might have been for a time, as to the preference of a Republican to a Kingly Government in their own case, they had the good sense and the good policy to spare the general leaning towards Kings which distinguished the rest of the world, and which, indeed, through the far greater part of their history, will be found to have distinguished themselves. I never read that they beat their foreheads in despair at the sight of the

insignia of Royalty, or appeared moonstruck
in the presence of a throne. No. They could
send out from the heart of Republican Rome
the prepared symbols of Royalty,—the ivory
sceptre, and the flowered robe,—and created
Kings by the sanction of public authority.
It was this sound management of the incli-
nations of society which laid the foundation
of their universal power—*hinc crevere opes.*
What becomes of your absurd Convention
of Royalty Haters, in comparison of these
King-making Republicans? The formation
of a circle of smaller Republics, all dependent
on the mother state, and looking to it as
their common centre, is the mad and impracticable resolve of France. Nay, Garat
will tell you that this is already done. " Dans
" les convulsions même de sa naissance, la
" Republique Française a semé partout des
" Republiques. Elle s'eleve au milieu d'elles,
" comme une mère immortelle entourée d'en-
" fans immortels." This is at once falsehood
and bombast. But what was the practice of

Rome? Cicero shall tell you in the case of Deiotarus. Was Deiotarus compelled to change
his ancient form of government, to call primary assemblies, and fling his regal authority
at their feet? did the Romans melt down his
crown, and, in its stead, fix a red cap on his
indignant brow? and did they style him
Citizen Deiotarus? and did they break
open his jails, and let out the patriot ruf-
fians in aid of morality and legislation? and
did the poor man lose all his patience, and
secretly vow to take the first moment of
vengeance which a reverse of things might
offer?—No. Rome bade him reign, and
confirmed the royal succession in his son.
What was the consequence?—That gratitude
and attachment, which contributed, with
other measures of similar policy, to the establishment of Rome's universal empire. Deiotarus saw all that was precious to him in the
preservation of his Kingly Office; and his
conduct towards his mighty benefactors
(who might have disposed of him in a dif-

ferent manner), was proportioned to their
sage indulgence of his ancient feelings.—
" Omnia tu Deiotaro tribuisti, cum et ipsi
" et filio Nomen Regium concessisti. Hoc
" nomine retento atque conservato, nullum
" beneficium populi Romani, nullum judi-
" cium de se Senatûs imminutum putat."
Cicero could lawfully plead the cause of
this King in the midst of Rome, and testi-
fied the public sanctity which the regal title
had always obtained there.—' Semper Re-
" gium Nomen in hac civitate sanctum fuit."
What now becomes of the clamours of the
French tribune against the names and offices of all Kings? How will they stand a
comparison with this patronage of the throne
constitutionally undertaken by the greatest
of the Roman orators? and what will be
the ultimate effect of these groans and
hisses, as absurd as they are indecent? I
bless God, that, amid the great mischief
which the French have been permitted to
work in the world, their malignant influ-

ence carries about it every appearance of its own speedy destruction. They are too infatuated, too selfish, too bigotted, and too ignorant to hold the earth in durable chains. Whatever evil has hitherto been done, has arisen from the mere force of the vicious principles of which they have declared themselves the patrons. Their own disgustful mode of propagating their doctrine will, by and by, be the effectual antidote to it. The scorpion which stings, affords the cure of its own poison; and I look forward to the time (not long hence) when Europe shall recover from the temporary consternation into which she has been thrown;—wonder that even a transient submission should have been given to so revolting a proselytism;—shake herself from the last remnant of Gallic pollution, and see all her public and private functions proceed in their accustomed order—*redeunt Saturnia regna.*

I will briefly instance another point of difference in the policy of the two Republics.

I need not repeat what French insanity has
dictated on the important subject of Religion:
the bloody proscription of its ministers,
with whose miseries all Europe groans ; and
the impious mockery of every thing sacred,
distinguish these cruel and ill judging legislators. The altar and the throne are
equally outraged ; and they provoke at
once the arm of power, and the tongue of
doctrine against them. What of the Romans?—If there was any part of their conduct which, more than another, exhibited
the soundness of their public judgment, it was
their eminent zeal in the support of the best
religion which they knew, and the alliance
which they anxiously maintained between it
and the state. If it suited my views to be
so particular, I could convince you by an
adduction of passages from their writers,
indeed from Cicero alone, with what joy
they would have witnessed that superior
system, which it was reserved for their de-
scendants to embrace, and which, together

with every other, is now the derision of
France.—But in whatever sad condition religion lay, the Romans treated it as reve-
rentially as they could. The worship of
other countries obtained a general sanction
from them ; and while they kept up the due
performance of their national rites, they
knew how to win a foreign state by other
means than arms. From time to time they
incorporated an alien Deity, and gave it a
flattering rank in their ascendant calendar.
Even Egypt was not neglected ; and the
empire gradually rose by the solemn preservation of their paternal ritual, and a well-
timed condescension to the objects of foreign
worship. The remains of Roman taste and
magnificence which, as a traveller, you must
know, are one grand comment on their religious propensities. Their historians, their
orators, and critics, are full of the pomp of
sacrifice, the sacred priests, and the reference
of their political measures to the sanction of
the Pontifices. In a subject so pregnant, it

would be needless to send you to the in-
numerable passages of Livy, of Cicero, of
Varro, or Gellius. The only quotation I
will use shall be from Valerius Maximus,
who attributes their empire to the grateful
return made by the Gods to Roman piety.
" Non mirum, si pro eo imperio augendo
" custodiendoque pertinax Deorum indul-
" gentia semper excubuit, quod, tam scru-
" pulosa cura, parvula quæque momenta Re-
" ligionis examinare videtur."* For the
rest, I refer you to Dr. Middleton's " Trea-
" tise of the Roman Senate," and particu-
larly to that part of it which immediately
follows his correspondence with Lord Her-
vey. You will there find, that it was not
only the office of the Senate to make Kings
(which was my first instance), but that it
was also vested with the guardianship and
superintendence of the public Religion. Yet
the French legislators think otherwise, and

* Lib. i. C. i.

hope to succeed ! They affect to insulate
their politics, and to make them stand without the indispensable aid of Religion ! Here
is another argument against their universal
empire.—They have not founded their state
fabric on the rock of human sentiment.
Like material fabrics built on sand, it must
fall, and " great will be the fall of it."

Observe, I pray you, another difference
in the limits of their respective legislation.—
When the Roman Senate met, they pro-
ceeded to deliberate like sensible men, not
on other people's business, but their own :
they made no sweeping declaration of universal and imprescriptible rights.—It was
enough for them if they considered what
was proper to be done for Romans—*quid
ex re sit populi Romani.* Nay, in the first
tumults attending the expulsion of the Tar-
quins (when, if at any time, violence was to
be expected) they well adapted their reso-
lutions to their immediate wants. Livy,
who only blames them for being somewhat

too punctilious in the mode of securing their
new constitution, gives, among other pru-
dential acts, this instance of their measured
conduct. The oath offered to the people
by Brutus himself did not overstep the limits
of their state : and though they were sur-
rounded with Kings, they said nothing
against them ; content with resolving that
no one should reign in *Rome——neminem
Romæ passuros regnare.* Yet Brutus is the
great object of French admiration.—They
wake and sleep with Brutus—they deck the
bust of Brutus with garlands ;—and, were
it not for Marat, Brutus might be a God !
But did Brutus aspire to legislate for his
neighbours ?—No. He left the Veians, the
Lavinians, the Tarquinians themselves to
have Kings or not, as they pleased. We see
then the solid proceedings of the Romans at
all times.—They won the nations to them
by abstaining from the apparent control
of their concerns, and obtained effectual
empire by seeming for a while to neglect it.

With what derision must a deep Senator of this stamp have looked upon an unconcocted and ever-meddling Conventionalist?—In the plenitude of his vanity, the Frenchman supposes the whole of mankind centered in his person! if he legislates, it is not for himself, but for all the world through him! He swells out the limits of his insufficient frame, and would be thought to carry a representative from all nations in his belly—the Englishman, the German, the Dutchman, the Caffrarian, the very Samoiede!——Is France to lay aside the government of a King?—universal nature abhors Kings. Is Paris to have a Mayor?—Mayors are convenient to the human race!——I would ask, is impudence and shallowness like this to hold the world in subjection?—No. Whatever ascendancy the violence of the moment has given them, their reign must be short. They go upon principles which shock all human feeling. They rush abroad with most offensive intrusion, and stir up against

them the self-love of every man's breast.
They are the only people on earth that
have no internal concerns !—

I could state other points of dissimilitude.
—I could contrast the French cupidity of territory, indulged amid the grossest inconsis-
tencies, and the violation of every pledge solemn or sacred, with the wholesome declaration of the wiser Romans. Valerius Maximus
will again afford you an example in the person of Africanus.* When at a sacrifice, the
usual prayer was offered for prosperity to
Rome and enlargement of its empire. "Hold,"
said he, " the empire is large enough ; I pray
" for the continuance of what we already
" possess." And we are told, that the Cen-
sors from that time adopted this temperate
request—*votorum verecundia.* It is true, the
Romans themselves deserted this principle.
But when ?—when they began to have their
Jourdans (*coupe-tête*) and their Buonapartes.

* Lib. 4. C. 1. 10.

But mark—before this took place, public virtue was gone.

I could state to you a farther difference in the treatment of allies, a word sacred in the acceptation of every good Roman. I have already quoted a passage from Cicero, expressive of their reverence for the Kingly Name. He very emphatically adds, that of their allies, " Semper Regium Nomen in hac " civitate sanctum fuit ; sociorum vero Re- " gum et amicorum, sanctissimum." In another place, he tells you what had been the sacred caution of their ancestors in this respect, amid the tumults of war itself.* And in his own age (grown so licentious) he honourably states concerning his favourite commander, that the peaceful territory which he crossed to get at the enemy, bore not the least mark of rapacity, no vestige of injury, " Cujus legiones sic in Asiam per- " venerunt, ut non modo manus tanti exer-

* Pro Lege Man.

" citûs, sed ne vestigium quidem cuiquam " pacato nocuisse dicatur." What, after this, will be said of a French leader, who indiscriminately sacks the cities of friends and foes ?—let the tears and groans of Genoa, of Tuscany, of Venice, testify the cruel folly which marks their treatment of allied or neutral states. Trojan or Tyrian, no matter : their impartial iniquity oppresses all alike. It is true, the Romans themselves, deserting the maxims of their forefathers, fell into the same injustice. And so Cicero tells you. But when ?—not till public virtue was declining, and the empire had become the prey of ambitious and desperate factions.

It is this decay of all good principle which furnishes what resemblance may be found between the Romans and French. " France " in her cradle displays the vices of Rome in " her decrepitude." There spoke truth, though from a French mouth. Dumouriez was right : and it is only in the disgraceful

F

or iniquitous parts of their mutual history, that the similitude will hold. Sometimes a Claudius was found, who, when the sacred chickens refused to eat, drowned them by way of making them drink. The *civic baptism* of the recusant priests, deridingly given by drowning, sufficiently declares the impious alliance. *Et documenta datis, quâ sitis origine nati.* But still there is a difference in favour of the Romans. Claudius was but one. The people trembled at this infidel joke, they imputed the subsequent loss of their fleet to it, and condemned the sneering Consul. What of the French ?—Either they looked on, and applauded the impious merriment, or never interposed in a body to punish it.

Clodius again (they never get out of the filthy track of a Claudius or a Clodius). Clodius, I say, was their great prototype in pugnacious legislation. Their deliberative wisdom dwells in their fingers. Who but must see the fury of the French tribune ; its clamours, its collarings, and its fistings, in the ever memorable violence of the Clodianites; in their blows and spittings on the Pompeians, till their misbegotten leader was kicked out of the Rostra?—" Clodiani " nostros *consputare* cœperunt, factus a nos- " tris impetus, ejectus de Rostris Clodius,'' &c. I recommend to your Lordship's admiration the whole of this legislative combat, as described by Cicero,* in an indignant letter to his brother. And with this I take my leave of the subject, disgusted and tired with scene upon scene of impiety and absurdity; all the good omitted, the evil diligently preserved and aggravated.

I have been so far employed in shewing your Lordship that your favourite Frenchmen resemble only the corrupt part of the Romans. Whether in the frantic disruption of the established laws, or in the unprincipled triumph of a never ending demagogism, the likeness thrusts itself upon me.

* Lib. 2. 3.

But where is their sage legislation, and their
virtuous heroism? I can trace them in the
filth of a Clodius, or the fury of a Cataline:
but where are the Catos and the Scipios?—I
know the futile people of Paris have flatter-
ed themselves with the possession of each
great character. Through the spectacles of
their levity they have seen the one in the
quondam shoe-strings of Roland, and the
other in the air of Truguet. Truguet declares himself a hero, and a modest hero.
Long live Scipio of the Marine! Roland's
white head is without powder. Long live
Roland of Utica!—*Ohe! jam satis est.*

This Roman affinity being disproved, I
might at once put an end to an Address already too long.—But I will beg one last moment of your attention to a true resemblance
nearer home. Will your Lordship be angry
to be told, that your admired Revolutionists
of the present day exhibit over again the
quondam Puritans of our own country?
If you wonder that men of such different

views can be compared together, it is easy
to solve your doubt.   Not to mention the
proverbial meeting of extremes, the difference is not so great as you imagine between
the two parties. Hostility to the throne was
essential to the success of both ; and those
who would discard all religion, are not far
removed from the bigots who proscribed all
but their own. Though, in this instance,
the ultimate object was not the same, the
previous means were perfectly alike ; and
both sides were united in the destruction of
the existing establishments. The *impious* and
the *elect* march hand in hand, and afford a
curious similarity of action.

Before the Democratic leaders in either
nation can introduce themselves to power,
they must endeavour to discredit the old
system. Accordingly, the press is let loose ;
and, with the infamous license of the Jacobins, we can compare the " noise and fury
" of the Puritans—their seditious zeal, and
" calumny against the existing authorities."

The sanctity that hedges the throne must be broken through by the odium excited against its administration. Accordingly, the French Assembly was inundated with false petitions (procured by its own corruption), for the redress of ten thousand alleged grievances. And what was it but the same spirit which impelled the Long Parliament (rejoiced at its successful tampering with the public), to divide into *forty committees*, sitting at one time, to consider of certain imaginary wrongs, against which they had procured remonstrances from the people? Mark too the miserable persons from whom both parties were glad to obtain petitions:—ever memorable is that of the London beggars, that the " Lords " would sit with the Commons, and vote as " one body."—Equally memorable is that of the women, headed by the brewer's wife, concerning the equal right they had of " de-" claring their sense of the public cause." Did not the Commons in a body thank the beggars? and did not Pym go out in person to

the women, and thank them too? Who does
not see, in these instances, the intrigues
which produced the union of the " Third
" Estate," with the Nobles and Clergy in
one house (the signal of ruin to France),
and the complacency of the demagogues to
Mademoiselle Theroigne on horseback, at
the head of the petitioning prostitutes, and
fishwomen of Paris?—It is to be observed,
that the women were powerful engines in
the hands of the Revolutionists on either
side of the water. We all remember the do-
nations on the loaded table of the Assembly ;
the patriotic offerings of the French females;
and their fingers stripped of their silver
thimbles for the good of the state. In the
same manner we find that, at the bringing
in of the plate for the service of the Parliament, there was not room to bestow it ; and
the women brought their " silver thimbles
" and bodkins to support the good cause."
The rage for proselytism we find to be pre-
cisely the same in the Puritan and the Jaco-

bin; and they both remind me of a passage
in Thucydides, concerning some of the people
affected with the plague, which he so well
describes. The malady, it seems, gave them
a strong dislike to being alone. They were
never easy till they got into company; and
never more delighted than when they found
a convenient opportunity to infect others,
sparing neither friends nor relations! Would
not one swear that there was a correspondence of affection between the mind and the
body, and that the one has its equal set of ail-
ments to match the stock of the other? The
never-ending encroachments on the Sovereign were of a like stamp in both countries.
How did the oppressed heart of Louis revive
for a moment, when a deputation from the
Assembly came to offer him their homage
for his acceptance of the constitution? Did
not Charles equally hope, that by consent-
ing to the bill, so long urged upon him, for
triennial Parliaments, he had fully satisfied
those who solemnly thanked him for it?—

Unhappy men ! it was no single measure, of whatever kind, that would satisfy the enemies of either. They must be in their graves, that revolutionary iniquity may have its free course.

    " And shall we kindle all this flame,
    " Only to put it out again :
      " And must we now give o'er,
    " And only end where we begun ?
    " In vain this mischief we have done,
      " If we can do no more."

Denham sung for more than his own age and nation.

Who but must think of the Brissotine cabinet forced upon the indignant King of France in the persons of Roland, Claisere, &c.; when he hears the project of appointing Hollis to be Secretary of State to Charles, and Pym, Chancellor of the Exchequer ?— But this was tolerable in comparison of what followed. Who but must weep at the indignities offered to the offspring of both the royal families ; the vile superintendence of Simon over the Dauphin, and the vulgar scheme of binding the Duke of Gloucester apprentice to a mechanic, and the Princess Elizabeth to a button-maker? Fortunately, the Princess died : the Prince was transported. They were indeed the levellers of both parties who proposed these last schemes.— For in revolutions things generally go from bad to worse. The engineer deservedly hoists with his own petard ; and, by the vengeance of Heaven, their more furious successors cut off without remorse the earlier fomenters of disturbance. A Girondist is the proper food of a Jacobin, as a Presbyterian was of the Independent or Millenarian—

> " Ætas parentum, pejor avis, tulit
> " Nos nequiores, mox daturos
> " Progeniem vitiosiorem."

Their legislative attempts, when both parties were in possession of power, are strikingly alike. Mark their common tyranny. The English Parliament voted not to dissolve themselves, but to fill up the house by new elections. The self-continued power of the

two thirds of the French Convention is a
near copy of this Democratic stretch. Mark
their common injustice. Above one half of
the established Clergy in England were turned out. to beggary and want, for no other
crime than their adhering to the civil and
religious principles in which they had been
educated. Wherever the Puritan armies came,
the officers preached (for there were no chap-
lains), and they turned the Churchmen out of
their pulpits, to deliver their own orations.
And Barebone's Parliament abolished tithes
and the clerical function altogether. To
aid the revenue of the usurpation, seques-
trations were adopted; estates of delinquents,
and church lands, were sold at low rates ;
the royal palaces were pulled in pieces, and
the materials turned into money. It is needless to adduce similar instances from France.
They will occur to the mind of every reader
without farther suggestion. Mark, again,
their common cruelty. The infernal decree
of the Jacobins, that quarter should be re-

fused to the English and Hanoverians, is not
without a precedent. During their contest
with the English King, the Parliament actually voted, that no quarter should be given
to the Irish who had joined the Royal standard! Mark, again, their common absurdity:
compare the French civic fasts (till the calves
patriotically hastened to become bullocks)—
with the request of the Parliament to the
people of England, that they would fast one
day in the week, and give the savings to the
public purse. Compare too the total alteration of the French Calendar, their decades,
and sansculotides—with the abolition, by
Parliament, of all the usual holidays, and
the setting apart of the second Tuesday in
every month for recreation. No matter what
the alteration is. The usual recollection of
mankind must be unhinged in small things
as well as great. I could select a volume of
this sort, were I not obliged to be rapid.
One more instance shall suffice—the final
assault on the throne. It has been observed

that the bringing of the English King to justice (as they termed it) struck in with the prevailing notions of the equality of mankind, and insured the devoted obedience of the army. This has been exactly repeated in France. The bulletin of Louis's health reported from the Temple to the Convention, is but a copy of the affectation of the Parliament, who published from time to time intelligence of what they termed the King's good condition, his cheerfulness, &c. while a prisoner in the Isle of Wight. The condemnation of both Sovereigns, in spite of justice, is the same ; and so is the surrounding of the scaffold with soldiers in such quantities, that the people, removed to a great distance, might not hear them speak. It has been said that the drums were beat at the execution of Louis. This I have reason to doubt ; though I have heard of punishments inflicted on the non-performance of the orders given to that effect. Be this as it may, the object in both cases was alike, to prevent the feelings of either people from being touched by the dangerous appeal of the Sovereign. I will not pursue this horrid parallel farther; though I might adduce a great number of additional instances. I leave them to be appreciated by those who are acquainted with the blackest portion of our own history, and will compare it with the existing revolution in France.

I am now satisfied. I have endeavoured to discharge my duty to those who are committed to my care. In reaching my parishioner, I have indeed taken upon me to expose the error of your Lordship's opinions. But the fault is your own. You ought not to have misled him. If, however, in the prosecution of the argument, I have expressed myself in any unbecoming way towards you, I shall acknowledge myself blameable. Yet feeling a high degree of constitutional reverence for the illustrious order to which you have the honour to belong, and comparing my sentiments with

the personal conduct which you have be-
trayed, I may perhaps be pardoned, if a
momentary warmth has stepped into the
gap which I discover between your senatorial duty and your political perverseness.
—At parting, I will leave with you a word
of advice.   I have heard you commended in
more than one Republic.   But allow me to
remind you, that the affectation of foreign
praise, to the neglect of home applause, is
pitiful indeed.   Every man's chief concerns
are in his own age and nation.   Suffer yourself to be commended in your proper country,
where alone your character is understood.
Be not forward to vulgarize your name with
every Titius or John Doe that blots the revolutionary list.—Be Earl Stanhope.—Be
a dignified and enlightened Peer.   Perform
your duty to the Constitution ;—and look
with due reverence to the Throne ; for from
thence alone springs the high consideration
of society towards you.

I am, &c.

FINIS.

www.ingramcontent.com/pod-product-compliance
Lightning Source LLC
Chambersburg PA
CBHW020328090426
42735CB00009B/1450